This Is the Ship I Used to Be

Poetry

Jonathan Humanoid

ARROYO SECO PRESS

© 2024 Jonathan Humanoid

All rights reserved for the author.
Please contact the author for permissions.

Logo by Morgan G Robles
morganrobles.carbonmade.com

Editor: Aruni Wijesinghe

Arroyo Seco Press

www.arroyosecopress.org

Cover art: cover image by BarbaraALane from Pixabay

ISBN: 979-8-9895659-1-7

This book wouldn't be possible without my mom. She's supported me and believed in what I've tried to do throughout my life. Special thanks to all three of the idiots at Two Idiots Peddling Poetry. The community they've created is something special. I'm grateful to have a space where I can be myself and be embraced in all of what that means. To anyone who has ever taken the time to read my work or listen to what I've shared, thank you. I only hope to be able to keep doing this for as long as I'm able to. Gratitude for being a part of my journey helping me walk my path.

Poems

To Break What Isn't Fixed 1
this poem used to be 4
Ending Cycles 5
Friendships Have to Be Easier Than Math, Right? 7
Maybe *This* Is the Year I Figure It All Out 9
Althazagoraphobia 12
An Easier Life Where We Are Both Cows 14
this poem used to be 17
How to unbury yourself—an epitaph in reverse 18
In Which I Am Still Alive and So Close to Finally Being
Glad That I Am 20
this poem used to be 22
In Response to Being Ghosted 23
From the Wreckage 25
I've Cracked So Many Eggs 28
this poem used to be 29
The Sun Will be In the Same Place No Matter What
Tomorrow Is 30
This poem used 31
this poem 32
this poem used to be 33
Phantom Limb Syndrome 34
To Be Something New 37
This Poem Is Future Tense 39
this poem used to be 41
On Remembering to Be 42
this poem used to be 43
This Is What I Was Built From, and Rebuild Myself From 44
Biography iii

To Break What Isn't Fixed

The Ship of Theseus paradox
asks this question about identity:
if you replace every part of a ship
will it still be fundamentally the same.

For as long as I can remember I've felt
I have been drifting without guidance,
surrounded by fog when the sea should be calm.
I have heard the murmurs of ghost, of curse—

I fear being the thing
that keeps people at a distance.
All I've ever wanted was a crew;
I was built with love by uncertain hands.

I have made myself of old memories.
What am I without all of this doubt?
I have replaced my emptiness with cannons—

there are way too many of them
and in places they shouldn't be.
They are heavy and I am sinking.
I have carried them in case I need them

but I never have.

What have I given up
in order to be what I think
someone else wants me to be?

What parts of myself became
something else
when I thought that they no longer worked?

I have believed if someone loved me
then I would be deserving of love.
This is another paradox:
I am made of them
and things I've needed to survive—
all a few strong waves
away from exploding.

I have loved suspiciously,
my legs wobbly
on unfamiliar ground.

Replace that with trust.

I have fucked like my being
deserving of love depended on it.
Replace that with connection.

When a relationship ended
I was left with an invoice
of the broken parts of me
that I felt I needed to replace.

I haven't known who I am
in such a long time;
I am a stranger in my own company.

A ship without repairs loses its purpose.
Maintenance is needed to keep it on the sea.

What does this metaphor become
if I trust myself to captain this ship?
What do I become if I define myself?

I make repairs to heal:
this is growth
It is progress
I am different
I am new
I am me.

There is work left.
There is love in that.

this poem used to be

a nightmare

lunar lucidity

        veiled vision
        prowling beast

           by day
           I feared few things

                in the dark
                I feared everything
                that I imagined

Ending Cycles

During the neurology appointment
that will determine whether my dad
meets the requirements for dementia
they ask him a series of questions:

How is his memory affected?
How does that affect his life?
They ask me to confirm what he says.
He tells them he can't remember

his mother's name and I wait
like I waited the day before
when he told me how angry
he still was and I listen now

as he tells them how much
he misses her, how he tried
to call her and I wait, don't
mention he barely called her

when he still could, so I know
this one isn't really a memory thing.
I remind him of our conversation.
He smiles sheepishly as I imagine

he did when he was the age
that he is digging up from
the graveyard of memories
that are always there but never

spoken of, at least not out loud.
My dad exhumes his mother's name
from one of these graves, and the dirt
from it is fresh. I can see it in his eyes.

He holds onto his anger silently.
This is how I know he still holds her.
The grave next to this one has earth
that hasn't been disturbed yet.

He has buried the relationship
that he wished they could have had.

He tells me he's glad I went with him:
I can see his hands holding the moment.
I am trying to accept the relationship
that we have, and the one we never will.

Friendships Have to Be Easier Than Math, Right?

Let x = who we are as individuals. Variable of uncertainty as we navigate this world. Trying to find stability when we have had to adapt to accommodate for a lifetime lacking it. How do you solve for something you cannot define? Show your work.

Let y = what we are to each other. Our pasts creating magnetism that pulls in and pushes away. You are the closest I've ever felt to being understood and that makes our friendship the most important thing to me. Variable of doubt: mine, in myself. Missing component of my own reflection. Error. Value not found. Show your work.

Don't worry. There's no actual math involved in this. I just wanted to sound smart. I like when you look at me like I've said something smart or terribly illogical. Both make me smile.

Let z = unfair expectations. Cheese pizza is an unfair metaphor. For real. I'm lactose intolerant. I don't want to be this in your life. I know you don't want that from me. This metaphor has been a Chuck E. Cheese-themed pity party. All of the animatronics singing shit to me are versions of you that I've wanted you to be. I haven't been able to stomach that you aren't just an ideation.

Let this poem be an apology for that. I want to get to know you. You in all the ways you show up for me and when you need me to show up for you. I know we'll figure it out. Show your work.

I still have so much to figure out. I'm still navigating the world. There are variables I still don't have solutions for. You are a point of stability to me that makes sense. But I can't expect you to define me. I don't want to define you. Things are going to keep changing. The more we add/ subtract/ figure out the order/ live/ figure out what living means—the clearer this will be.

Listen, I think I want our friendship to be that menu you use to order Taco Bell. Customized. Some days will be different than others. Add something. Take something away that just isn't it for that day. I don't think we are something that needs to be solved. We aren't a math problem. You are you. I still have more to learn about what that means. I am me. I still have more to learn about what that means. I'm just glad I get to navigate this world with you. Show your work.

Maybe *This* Is the Year I Figure It All Out

Is this it for you? Is this all you'll ever do?
—*Buddy Wakefield*

Listen, can you hear how loud everything is?
It isn't ever quiet enough. I can't stop
thinking about all I have yet to do.
I still don't know what it is;
I just know that I want more.

Are you there, Margaret? It's not god.
I think, if we are all created in god's image
then I sometimes look familiar, but god does not.
Maybe you are god, Margaret. So many women
I've loved and known have carried god in all the light in
them,

fragments of stars. Guidance.
A path. Proof of life.
Illumination in their existence.
Universe embodied
in their breath. I know
that I am connected to something –

honestly, I'm pretty high right now
but I'm still fairly certain of this:
Are you there, Margaret?
It's your Uber Eats driver.

Listen, your food is getting cold.
The mashed potatoes speak for themselves
and I don't know the language. So,
it's just nonsense. Listen. Do you understand
what they're trying to say?

So many cultures have a god of the harvest;
I am trying to remember how many
have a god of starvation. It feels like so many
of us are hungry but more of us are praying.
Maybe I should pray to you, Margaret.
I'm only an Uber Eats Driver in the fictional
situation I've created for this poem.

I don't drive.
My anxiety has kept that from happening
for the better part of the last 25 years.

Listen, is the world getting louder?
Even the job in this poem
is fictional. I'm going to be 40
in a few months. And the uncertainty
of everything I keep thinking gets louder
and louder. Listen, I don't know what to pray for.

I am god, but only if my image is one of those
magic eye images, where everything is shapeless
unless you stare at it real close, focus, then pull
your attention back. Maybe I'll find god if I focus
longer on the nonsense. Maybe neither of us is god,

or all us might be god and everyone is trying

their best to figure out how to be both imperfect
and in charge of themselves.
Doesn't that sound like a lot of pressure?

I'm really high right now for inspiration.
And you might think *Inspiration for what?*
All that you're doing is staying alive.

Some days I cannot imagine myself happy.
Some days I try and there is no image found
when I search for myself. Some days all I can do
is imagine something that could make me happy
and I am fighting for a day when I am too busy
living and failing and failing and failing and learning
and making slow progress in all   of   that
to notice that I've found some sort of purpose.

I can't keep being too busy daydreaming.
One day I will be in the moment
unconcerned with what could
make me happy.

And the moment is
and I am.
I am here.

Are you there?
I ate your food
while I was waiting.

Althazagoraphobia

I like words, knowing what they mean, figuring out
how they fit together with other words to form a sentence.
Create a line of poetry, build a stanza, like forming Voltron
from the individual mecha warrior lions. I like the power of
words.

I don't like small talk
        people trying to figure out who I am
like dissection
        or chopping up ingredients
                to make a meal.
And here, if meal is a metaphor   for knowing who I am

        then I am starving.

I am loud. Unless you count the thread
I have forced my quiet with.
Sewn shut. Sloppily. I do not
                        know how to work a needle.

Imagine the most beautiful museum you can think of.
There is a room filled with paintings, open to subjective
reaction. I am the murmured interpretations. All of them.

There was a time when if you asked, you would hear the echo
of someone else's words, said in love, said in criticism.
Who I am was an echo of how someone else saw me,
like footsteps that matched the steps I took, as if they were my own.

If you took a row of trees struggling in a storm,
branches scraping against each other, leaves thrashing,
and stuck all of that in the high-ceilinged exhibit room
filling quickly with impolite attempts at shushing—

I am loud like that.
I do not like quiet.
It gets too quiet sometimes
                    and my thoughts get so much louder.

I find myself forgetting
if I was ever anything else but the harshness
                        of all this being.
                    I am
                            forgetting
                                    myself.

An Easier Life Where We Are Both Cows

In an alternate universe
I do not tell her that I like her.
My words hang forever on my lip
like frostbite or something sweet
spilled from my tongue, chewed clumsily
and I am too embarrassed to wipe it away.

My feeling are parts of an ocean
trapped beneath the earth in a cave,
overwhelming in size at certain tides.
And there's a pirate ship filled with treasure

waiting
to be discovered.
Maybe she finds it,
but someone eventually will
when the tide is manageable.

There are an infinite number of alternate universes.
In some of them I tell her I like her;
she says *no* and I handle it well.
We're able to be friends and I like that.

In at least one we meet as cats or cows
in a much easier kind of life.

In all of the ones where I like her
the common thread is that I have
discovered myself before I realize that

maybe in another universe I figure out
what it means when she laughs at
all of my admittedly terrible jokes.
When she stops laughing, I see the boundary that sets.

In this universe we are waiting
on opposite platforms;
there are train tracks and silence.
The rumble of arriving and departing
lines of noise creates a vibration
that sounds like the words
I like you and I know enough
to not use metaphors or ambiguity.
She is so smart but that is not her strength.
Every now and then I can see her
and the empty space between us—
the distance
the lack of sound—
is too much.
There hasn't been a train
for all the sometime.
I avoid eye contact,
small rocks beneath my feet
that I don't have the energy
to kick away
shake in my line of sight.

There are no more trains
and neither of us has a destination.
I realize it is my body trembling
She cannot say anything.

I like you
buzzes in every rail,
electricity powering nothing.
I avoid eye contact for now,
kick the rocks to have something to do,
swallow the silence
a dry gulp.

Eventually I will look up.
I care about her as a person—
that matters more than my feelings.
In this universe I accept what can and cannot be.

this poem used to be
        rumination

            it was reflective
            (so I've been told)

                a single breath
                        lightning
                    for every thought
                                thunder

                            turned synapses
                                into storm

How to unbury yourself—an epitaph in reverse

4. At my funeral they all say beautiful things about me / they mean them / gray clouds linger above / there are tears / but no rain / yet flowers bloom / surrounding the tombstone / planted / thriving / there are bouquets of flowers / dead / dug up for this moment / placed gently on the tombstone / by hands that touch my name / fingers become bridges / between their world / and where I have gone / connection / the writers half-laugh / half-sob at the epigraph / Vonnegut / you know the quote / the writers know the irony / in everything being beautiful / nothing hurting / if we hit rewind on this scene / I would look like a flower blooming / dirt undug / my loved ones carrying a coffin / walking backwards / until the coffin is empty / and I am not / until the coffin becomes a tree / I am reading beneath

3. Before the person is buried / you must make sure they are dead / there is endless zombie fiction about this / but it is also true / before the seed is planted / you must make sure the soil is alive / to bury / to plant / you dig / you dig / the earth is disturbed / my grave undug / the dead flowers lain upon it / planted in living soil / breathing, stretching towards the sun / the people who loved me / do not speak of me in the past tense / they all say beautiful things about me / they mean them / they say them / because I do not believe the truth in their eyes / I am doing my best to bloom

2. When planting / when living / it is best to provide nutrients / flowers need sun, water, energy / all buds and green / small struggling / their unbloomed petals not believing the beautiful things / that the sun has to say about them / I see

coffin shapes in the graying clouds / dark of sky / tears open / I tilt my head to the sky / the liquid on my face is one / I cannot tell the source of drops / the epitaph carved into my skin / is washed away / drops collect in the crevice / between my lightly fluttering eyes / and the bridge of my nose / behind the fog of my glasses / in the dimples that only show when I smile / this becomes an epitaph for my unburial / an anthem for living

1. If you want a flower to grow / you must first plant a seed / I plant them in graveyards / where life is needed / I carve into existence / a belief in myself / strong as stone / I am growing / I have rooted / I am living, stretching towards the sky, patient / I plant loving words within myself / nurture them / I am growing / and the sky, I tell myself / always looks about ready to rain

In Which I Am Still Alive and So Close to Finally Being Glad That I Am

I used to tell people that my biggest fear
was that I would die alone and the dying
was something I was fine with being inevitable.
I was actually lower tier level afraid of getting old.

Secondary fear was snakes and the worst thing
I could possibly imagine was getting bit
on some beautiful trail in a majestic forest,
attention confused on my surroundings.

Dying alone meant never falling in love.
I don't think I really appreciated the people
who had loved me in a different way;
I felt alone and the world felt distant.

If everyone I loved left the room I would
be without anyone who loved me, even though
I was still in the room and I can't do math
but some part of that never seemed to add up.

All decomposition of the living.
All waiting for the living to stop.

What am I if I build myself into a home?
What have I been but a pack of cards
stacked up in the shape of a house,
all lacking in sturdy foundation?

How often have I fallen apart,
how many times have I stayed scattered?

The hours I have left on skip
are a blur of malevolent screams.
There are years of disembodied pacing,
footprints worn into floors of my apartment.

I cannot get back the time I have haunted
the places I thought I would never leave alive.

What am I if I am not yet dead?
My biggest fear is now letting the time
that I have left to be alive slip through my fingers —
I want to live like I love myself enough to flourish.

this poem used to be
        a   ghost

           howling
              my name
              like a demonic Pokémon.
              There was a time
              I entered rooms
                  as lamentation.
                      Sorrow stained
                  wall papers before
                      benevolence
                necromanced into
                      warmth of laughter.

In Response to Being Ghosted

I try to convince my friend
to embrace the role
as a form of healing.
I look up houses for sale
that have all been abandoned,
buy supplies from Michaels
to make us look the part
and head over a little after midnight.

We enter through a creaking wooden entrance
that leads us into an empty basement.
Our voices echo off the cement walls
and we let everything out of our lungs.
Properly attired and fully slaying the cosplay
we float from room to room loudly lamenting
the texts that still show they were left on read.
In the slivers of light sneaking into the living room
through cracks in the blinds, she is almost transparent.
Her words are still solid and sharp. *People suck.* She hurls
this at the floor; she appears to float further away from it.

I tell her that we are not haunting, that we are deserving this
      space.
She reminds me that technically what we are doing
is actually breaking and entering and I ramble past
her terribly logical point by distracting with the reveal of my plan
to get over this heartbreak. I ignore how noticeably she cringes.

So love is dead, right? She nods and I point out that we are dead;
by the transitive properties love is sure to find us now.
She tries to point out that this is not how any of that works,

but a third voice interrupts her. A man is standing there
You are not ghosts, he repeats. I look at my friend, forgetting
that ethereal beings don't have physical forms.
I move my shoulders in a shrug.

We're both confused by the accusation in his tone.
He moves towards us aggressively, rattling off
a list of ghost hunter shows I've only heard of
as evidence of his expertise on the subject.
He has watched them all and is offended
at the inaccuracy of our portrayal of something
he is so passionate about. I shrug again,
ask why he's there and he remembers himself
long enough to blink calm back into the tension of his body.
There is an open house this morning.
My friend and I have been ghosting and talking
the entire night. We stay for the food,
the social interaction. I have several conversations
that may or may not go anywhere
if I wasn't a ghost. But I am, so I don't worry about it.

My friend finds a group of college students
who are planning on renting the space together.
We mingle until she returns to stand next to me.
I can feel her head rest against my shoulder and I know
before she says anything that she is feeling human again,
and that might actually be more than she can handle right now.

As we are leaving the man from before shouts after us,
says that we are better at pretending to be alive than dead.
He does not mean this as a compliment
but I choose to take it as one.

From the Wreckage

When I was a kid, we used to spend a lot of summers
and winter breaks at my grandpa's house.
Sometimes my aunt would pick us up from school
and everything would already be packed,
and sometimes I found out we were leaving as we were leaving.

Because we hadn't seen my mom's family in a while.
Because this time she was actually leaving my stepdad, right?

My grandpa's house was about a half-mile from the border of
    Mexico.
There was a field behind it that stretched forever between
two lands.
It got quiet hours before it was time to go to bed.

I always had trouble falling asleep there.

I would listen for the sounds of the city,
my ears strained for the sound of a man's anger,
tsunami in his eyes despite the calm of his surface.

It was a different kind of quiet.

Some days I look in the mirror
and see Bud's aftermath in my irises.
I, too, am a storm building in the discomfort
of silences that feel like they say too much
about me, the way he saw me.
I see myself and fear anyone who loves me will, too.

Some days I see my mother's pain,
how she was losing her vision
while feeling like she was losing her son.

Some days I see the tension of my body language
and only realize now that my mother
may not have seen the evidence of destruction,
internal or external, that was there in quiet rooms.
That our house just started to default to after
all of the emergency alerts and screaming stopped.

Some summers we spent more time
in Tecate than we did at home.
Even then I knew what waited for us
returning to Bud was at least a familiarity.

What do you do with the wreckage of something
when you have never had time between events
to take the opportunity to rebuild?

I do not think
I have loved
any of the women
that I told my friends about.

I've been recreating
something familiar
but I'm recognizing the difference.
My friends are what makes me
certain that I do know what love is.

I am trying to be a home
for myself so I belong somewhere.
I've been single for a while now.
I'm learning to be comfortable with own company.
I am shaping myself and I recognize
myself most days.

My days are filled
with moments of quiet—

what a blessing it is
for that to mean peace.

I've Cracked So Many Eggs

I'm not sure I know how to make an omelet. Cooking for myself has been guessing and hope for longer than I have lived alone. There never seems to be the right ratio of eggs to everything else. What should be melted isn't, what shouldn't be liquid is, and more than once there has been a thick enough layer of some mysterious texture burnt onto the surface of the eggs, leaving a sort of light, plastic blanket keeping them warm.

Usually what makes it out of the pan just falls apart on the plate. I'm pretty sure omelets are meant to be comforting fluff folding other yummy things neatly into an embrace holding it together. I don't know what I end up making, but it is a pile of ingredients that I have guessed at the necessary time and temperature to cook. It becomes the culinary equivalent of Mortal Kombat. I hope with each bite whatever makes it out of the pan and into my stomach, my taste buds pleasantly surprised at the improvement of my skills.

I am still struggling to write happy poems because I am still figuring out what it means for me to be happy. What ingredients go together well enough? My joy is still caked in a thin layer of something a little bit burnt. I am grateful to not have to go hungry. What a blessing it is to be full.

this poem used to be
           a meal

                        Time was meant
                        to savor   yet it was
                        still   consumed

What it is to turn
     sustenance
              into
                 mindful
              indulgence

                   What is it
                   to be full?

The Sun Will be In the Same Place
No Matter What Tomorrow Is

You and I are staring at the same sky
squinting through open fingers
letting the sun settle on our skin.
Maybe we're seeing it at different times.

The sun is still there no matter
where on earth you are.
We are moving
closer or further away—

it's all about perspective.
I didn't understand the phrase
you can't love anyone until you love yourself
until I realized when someone did.

I had trouble believing I was deserving.
The sun will be there. You will be there.
This isn't a love poem
until it is. I won't be waiting for the turn.

This poem used
        to be a garden

        I think
        it forgot
        how to bloom

        rooted
        in concrete
always longing
        for what it lacks

                May it rain soon
                and stir up

                                the
                        scent of
                        soil

this poem

used to be

a photograph

I think there were people in it
at some point

I try
to remember
them
well
enough

to write
about

I can tell
we were
having fun

this poem used to be
a conversation
                        honesty has become
                        an alter ego

        stutter feelings into existence
                I say everything except what I mean

                        my words become boulders
        breaking against teeth

expecting to be cement mixed
                into poems

        the page fills
            I am full
        and still grasp at sounds

Phantom Limb Syndrome

For a long time your laughter
has been my laughter and on the days
that you smiled so did I,
my lips tugged gently upward,
and on the days you didn't
I always felt a little bit of panic.

Some days you remind me of everyone
I ever said *I love you* to in hopes one page
would be enough for us both to fit on.
Like if only I could take the sharp edges of us
and origami them into something we were part of.
There were never instructions and without actual skill

I just folded and folded until
all of our words were lost.

Some days you remind me of their absence
and the parts of myself still crushed into crumpled paper.

You met me at a time
when I was broken Buzz Lightyear,
entirely uncertain of who I was.
You were friend to me
when so much of how I survived
had been armored in anger and hurt.

When I didn't feel like anything else
you saw everything beneath
and I felt real as long as you were around.

I met you at a time when all of your feelings
were buried beneath a dragon behind your sternum,
safely guarded treasure I knew to keep my distance from.

I know you loved me,
but that felt inconsistent.

I know you didn't mean the fire
whenever we would get too close.

All of my feelings are flammable
and everything's been on fire for a while.

On the days when you talked about falling in love
with someone who began to drift into all
of our conversations, you would leave
on some Odyssean quest and I became a shore.

I never wanted you to love me in the same way.
I only ever wanted to be a place you felt safe to stay.

So much of our time together
became stories about this pursuit of glory —

you so often seeking it somewhere else,
me wanting to be a place of stability for my friend.

I know you loved me
but it felt like waves

guiding you back

or further away.

You can replace every part
of a ship and it is still a ship
whether it is something new or not.

I know I loved you
but I'm still struggling to love me.

There are too many metaphors in this poem.
I've used too many words to say *I love you,*
stay and *be my friend*. Stay. I've worked on myself
for you.

I won't be waiting anymore.
Maybe someday you'll listen
to the epic tale of how I found myself.

Someday I am going to smile naturally
and the pull at my lip won't feel foreign.
Someday I am going to laugh and the sound
won't have echoes of anyone else's voice in it .

I don't know who I am without
someone else loving me;
It's about time I become that person.

To Be Something New

I turned 40 today, and I was caught off guard by the smile that spread from my face to the day, and I almost panicked at how unfamiliar that was.

For years I have welcomed birthdays with a shrug; What I was doing barely felt like living, and so continuing to do that was met with indifference.

for a long time I have been a train barreling down an unfinished track with no attempt to decelerate into an actual destination. The negative thoughts I believed were fuel to maintain momentum, and the track was going to come to an end at some point. Or I was going to *Back-to-the-Future-III-* reference myself into the past to change all the lingering *what ifs.* Paradox myself into someone entirely different. Maybe then, I always thought, maybe then I would start living.

but this year has been a year of change. My priorities have shifted to focus on finishing the track, setting goals as stations I can aim to reach at speeds that feel more manageable. And what a difference it makes to life like you have time for living.

40.

I turned 40 today and I honestly never thought I would, but I'm grateful that I did, and there are more years and goals and people and places along this path.

I can't think of an antonym for indifferent right now, but it kind of excites me that there are still words that I will learn for the first time, that there's a world I will spend time in, a brief rest, or a short lifetime in that I have still yet to discover. It is so much bigger than me, but I turned 40 today and breathed its air into my lungs, and for the first time my chest didn't feel like a dying fire waiting for fuel to gain speed, to keep going, to keep pushing *I think I can, I think I can,* but I will in a time that is right for me.

This Poem Is Future Tense

I forget to breathe sometimes.
There's a Wilhelm Scream in my chest.
All my scars become fresh wounds.
My lungs are filled with a car crash
of my past and present colliding.
I am often afraid to open my mouth—
it feels like everyone I love will just leave.
When I manage to ask them to stay
my words are the shriek of metal on metal,
the aftermath of a wreckage
that is still happening in every moment I am in.

    A. I need to focus on myself no matter how much I
        like you.
    B. Time travel does not exist… yet. So, I need to be
        patient; there's trauma I still need to heal.
    C. If we can be anything we can't be anything right
        now.

This is probably a syllogism: I like you
like I like philosophical concepts.
I don't think I fully understand them
but I like them enough to keep trying to.
I like you enough to know that every moment
that is a moment you and I are in together
is quiet, is safe, is enough to keep me there.
It isn't only because of the feeling of repair,
of feeling good enough despite the damage.

I like you. I know that
when you look at me
and it takes my breath away.
I want my lungs to realize
this is how it is supposed to feel.
I want the temporary loss of breath
to be present tense. I'm not asking you to wait for me;
I'm not saying that I'm going to wait—

but if I love you,
it will be future tense.

this poem used to be
     an exit

     I no longer see it as an option;
     this road is long and I am realizing

          that I need to maintain myself
             in order to remain on the road
          to keep moving forward
          to keep living

          there are so many things I need
             to unlearn

there are so many things
     I still need to learn
          I wasn't expecting
        to be making this trip

     but what a blessing it is
for this to be such an adventure

On Remembering to Be

In old Germanic the word *mann*
referred to people in general.
The male version of this word
was *were,* and it lives on
only in the word *werewolf.*

I have stopped caring
if I have failed as a human,
or whether or not
I'm man enough.
I am greatly disappointed

that I might have failed
as a werewolf.

I never even got the chance
to see how well I might do,
and I would devour anyone
who laughed about

how many poems I have written
about the moon.

this poem used to be
        disheveled

                            so, I patched
                            it together

        chaos/excitement
        vulnerability/power
            misery/elation
                death/growth

                            anarchy/mindfulness
                            wandering/purpose
                            anger/survival

            my life/balance

This Is What I Was Built From, and Rebuild Myself From

Borderline personality disorder belongs to a family of diagnoses in the DSM that have a unique level of stigmatization. In the Venn diagram of nature versus nurture, the environmental affects circle would be larger than the hereditary/chemical circle. The overlap would come from the diagnosis being a tree whose roots crack sidewalks chaotic in their growth. It plants itself as a seed in the patient when they are still in the developmental stages of childhood.

Between the ages of five and seven, children develop their sense of self from the interactions with the adults around them. It is the foundation for personality and stability in attachment styles which help develop into concepts of healthy relationships as the child grows their sense of individuality and worth. So, if the interactions with the adults in the child's life are negative and we imagine the child as a house—there is no foundation. You cannot keep building on that. You cannot add new floors and expect stability. They will never feel as if they are a home for themselves, and you will endlessly search for that in people and things that feel like construction. All will be safety zones and fear of work site-related hazards. How else do things get built? And the child becomes an adult. There are so many half-finished buildings now. The billboard in front still says Work in Progress. The child remains incomplete.

This sense of emptiness is one of the main symptoms of borderline personality disorder. There are a few things to look for when diagnosis is considered. Splitting occurs with people, the patient feels close enough to want them to stay. Fear of

44

them leaving creates an intense game of teeter-totter in which they can bounce from idolizing the person on a level of infallibility to fearing abandonment and villainizing them. You wrap yourself in barbed wire (metaphorically) to control proximity (successfully). People still embrace you. This is confusing, but it feels nice. When the embrace ends—as all things end—you won't understand. The metal barbs have pierced you both. The pain feels literal.

An unstable sense of self is a long-term effect of the stages of development being skipped in childhood. You will be asked how you feel. This question is simpler than you make it. The frustration doesn't come from the emotion. You know what emotions have carved you into existence that day. It is the use of the personal pronoun—you. You do not feel real. You are a statue. Parts of you might be broken. You're not sure. You've forgotten the shape of yourself.

Emotional regulation occurs when the child learns to process emotion before reacting. Emotional dysregulation occurs in borderline personality disorder in instantaneously reacting to situations and interactions before processing cognitively and objectively the experience itself. Intense moods of hostility, euphoria, anxiety, and sadness can last for hours, days, or longer while processing happens. You are trying to remember what it is to be an ocean. You remember waves. You remember tranquility in the flow. You cannot remember when you felt that. You are a storm.

Sometimes you are a frightened child still. All you want is attention. You become self-absorbed. Where your empathy used to be an abundant well, you become cavernous. Provide nothing. Self-destruction and impulsivity are phantom limbs of your amputated belief in your own worth. You can feel the tingle of where your value has been severed. Ethereal fingers around your throat or pressing against your chest. A reminder that you do not feel deserving of happiness. A resuscitation of your joy. Hedonism. Danger. You indulge arrogantly. You grow to hate that you do not casually taste. You consume.

Treatment of borderline personality disorder sometimes includes medications. Long term therapy encourages mindfulness and dialectics. Challenge the negativity of the people who gave you rotten wood to build a home of yourself. Silence their voice. Rebuild yourself. You are enough. You are whole. You are complete. You are valuable. You always have been.

Biography

Jonathan Humanoid writes poems and is constantly confused. He would like to believe that the writing poetry thing helps with the being confused, but there's no evidence to support this. He writes in the hopes that others will feel less alone by reading his work as he feels less alone by sharing it.

Jonathan has had poems published in *Freeze Ray, Fight Evil With Poetry - Anthology Volume One,* and *Sh!t Men Say to Me: A Poetry Anthology in Response to Toxic Masculinity.* He likes making old-school DIY chapbooks and has released three so far called: *I Was Never Going to be Normal, How to Accept That Your Words Are Going to Outlive You,* and *All the Light in Me.* The collection *This Is the Ship I Used to Be,* which explores his experiences with Borderline Personality Disorder, is his first published full-length poetry.

Jonathan is grateful to have so many people who love him. He is glad to finally be one of those people.

Jonathan Humanoid offers readers passage on his journey into building and rebuilding a self and a life to be lived. Framing his search for self through metaphors of ships and storms, wreckage, and ghosts, he pulls us toward an understanding of what it means to craft a sense of belonging amidst impermanence.

In spite of its size, the collection explores the subject of self and progression through varying subject matter—navigation and traveling, graveyards and gardening, hunger and cooking, love and loving—with the "this poem used to be" poems charting a circuitous path. This is Margaret's answer not from god, but from an Uber Eats driver who got hungry while waiting.

Never didactic, *This Is the Ship I Used to Be* is all at once a late-night conversation between friends, philosophical discussions of time and meaning, geeky wordplay, lyrical confessions, and a promise of better to come.

—LeAnne Hunt

Jonathan Humanoid's *This Is the Ship I Used to Be* is a collection filled to the brim with warrior words. The unfinished roads to self-love and reinvention are so beautifully paved in the lines of these powerful poems, edited within an artfully structured narrative arc that takes you on an empowering journey. Humanoid's innovative, accessible poetry will resonate with readers and move them with its courage, humor, heart, and unflinching depth.

—Kevin Ridgeway, author of *Invasion of the Shadow People* (Luchador Press)

The route to healing can be a path of storms, where doubt of survival rears its head. Jonathan Humanoid takes us on a voyage, inviting readers to witness poetry of grief and growth. *This Is the Ship I Used to Be* is an honest reflection of a soul as it chooses the path of self-love, exploring what it truly means to be oneself in the face of constant change.

—Ellen Webre, author of *A Burning Lake of Paper Suns*

www.ingramcontent.com/pod-product-compliance
Lightning Source LLC
Chambersburg PA
CBHW070042110426

42741CB00036B/3233

9 7 9 8 9 8 9 5 6 5 9 1 7